THE REAL MEN in BLACK BEHIND THE BENDER MYSTERY

THE FBI FILE OF ALFRED K. BENDER

Kenneth Arnold

SAUCERIAN PUBLISHER

ISBN: 9798596181289

ISBN-13: 9798596181289
GTIN-14:09798596181289
© 2021, Saucerian Publisher

Prologue

It is generally a good idea to return to the classics in any genre. This also goes for UFO literature. Rereading a book after ten or twenty years is a rewarding experience. You will discover new data and ideas you didn´t notice before. The reason, of course, is that you are, in many ways, not the same person reading the book the second or third time. Hopefully you have advanced in knowledge, experience, intellectual and spiritual discernment. A good starting point is to reread the contactee classics of the 1950's, in order to understand the deeper mystery involved in what happened during that era.

Albert K. Bender was an American ufologist, and organizer of the Flying Saucer Bureau who claimed to have discovered important data on the origin of UFOs, but he was silenced in 1953 by the visit of three mysterious men dressed in black suits. Three years later, this story was released by publisher/writer Gray Barker in: *They Knew Too Much about Flying Saucers*. This book firmly established the MIB (Men in Black) legend among UFO believers. However, for believers, Men in Black are real. For non believers, these men are fictional characters. However, it is undeniable that some sort of secret agents, from the US Government, have questioned people that had experienced the UFO phenomena, because the government considered them a threat to national security. In Bender's case, the FBI investigated him. Here, Bender's FBI file is made public for the first time.

Saucerian Publisher was founded with the mission of promoting books in Ufology, Paranormal, and the Occult. Our vision is to preserve the legacy of literary history by reprint editions of books which have already been exhausted or are difficult to obtain. Our goal is to help readers, educators and researchers by bringing back original publications that are difficult to find at reasonable price, while preserving the legacy of universal knowledge. This book is an authentic reproduction of the original printed text in shades of gray. ***IMPORTANT**, despite the fact that we have attempted to accurately maintain the integrity of the original work, the present reproduction has missing and blurred pages, poor pictures and FBI censorship's pencil markings from the original scanned copy. Many of the original FBI documents pages are shadowy, and faint. **ILLEGIBLE PAGES HAVE A NOTE.** Because this material is culturally important, we have made available as part of our commitment to protect, preserve and promote knowledge in the world. Some of the issues could be missing. Great, but unpretentious, this edition is a rare symbols by itself of what was going in the begining of the modern UFO phenomena.This edition is a collection of documents regarding Benders' life, and has the following parts: 1.Introduction; 2. ALFRED K. BENDER'S PHOTOS; 3.ALFRED K. BENDER'S DOCUMENTS; 4.ALFRED K. BENDER'S NEWSPAPER ARTICLES; 5.Bender's FBI File.

Editor, Saucerian Publisher, 2021

INDEX

Introduction

In popular culture and UFO conspiracy theories, Men in Black (MIB) are supposed men dressed in black suits who claim to be government agents who harass or threaten UFO witnesses to keep them quiet about what they have seen. It is sometimes implied that they may be aliens themselves. The term is also frequently used to describe mysterious men working for unknown organizations, as well as various branches of government allegedly designed to protect secrets or perform other strange activities. The term is generic, used for any unusual, threatening or strangely behaved individual whose appearance on the scene can be linked in some fashion with a UFO sighting. Several alleged encounters with the men in black have been reported by UFO researchers and enthusiasts.

MIBs are popularly described as:
* Appearing in threes
* Ttravelling in large, black, old-model cars (usually Cadillacs in the USA), which appear to be brand new and have untraceable registrations
* Having 'dark' complexions
* Appearing only rarely outside the USA
* Possessing knowledge known only to the witness.

In general, the Men in Black (MIB) usually have one main purpose: to muzzle witnesses of strange, paranormal phenomena. They almost always wear black suits and hats with dark sunglasses, drive black cars and arrive in groups of two or three. Some describe them as one would an FBI agent, while others recall the MIB as having strange appearances, sometimes with supernatural features like glowing eyes and strange complexions.

The most celebrated MIB case was that reponed by UFO investigator and author Alben K. Bender. In 1953 he was allegedly 'silenced' by three MIBs.These men are not a myth, nor a folklore, they are really FBI agents.

The modern image of Men in Black started in 1947. 1947 is considered by most historians of the United States as the year when the Cold War began with the implementation of the "Truman Doctrine" to contain the propagation of world Communism, which give rise to the anti-communist hysteria of the following years. Also, 1947 was the year when the first UFO sightings were reported in the summer. Kenneth Albert Arnold was born on March 29, 1915 in Sebeka, Minnesota, and died on January 16, 1984 at the age of aged 68. He was the owner of Great Western Fire Control Supply in Boise, Idaho that sold and installed fire suppression systems. Also, as a result of the nature of his job that took him around the Pacific Northwest, he uses his experience as pilot to travel in a CallAir A-2 . On June 24, 1947, Arnold was flying

Incident
4AF 1208 I
16 July 1947

MEMORANDUM FOR THE OFFICER IN CHARGE:

1. On 12 July 1947, [redacted], Boise, Idaho, was interviewed in regard to the report by [redacted] that he saw 9 strange objects flying over the Cascade Mountain Range of Washington State on July 25th. [redacted] voluntarily agreed to give the interviewer a written report of exactly what he had seen on the above mentioned date. The written report of [redacted]s attached to this report as Exhibit A,

AGENT'S NOTES: [redacted] is a man of 32 years of age, being married and the father of two children. He is well thought of in the community in which he lives, being very much the family man and from all appearances a very good provider for his family. [redacted] has recently purchased a [redacted] recently purchased a [redacted] in which to conduct his business to the extent of which is explained in the attached exhibit. It is the personal opinion of the interviewer that [redacted] actually saw what he stated that he saw. It is difficult to believe that a man of [redacted] character and apparent integrity would state that he saw objects and write up a report to the extent that he did if he did not see them. To go further, if [redacted] can write a report of the character that he did while not having seen the objects that he claimed he saw, it is the opinion of the interviewer that [redacted]s in the wrong business, that he should be writing Buck Rogers fiction. [redacted] is very outspoken and somewhat bitter in his opinions of the leaders of the U.S. Army Air Forces and the Federal Bureau of Investigation for not having made an investigation of this matter sooner. To put all of the statements made by [redacted] in this report would make it a voluminous volume. However, after having checked an aeronautical map of the area over which [redacted] claims that he saw the objects it was determined that all statements made by [redacted] in regard to the distances involved, speed of the objects, course of the objects and size of the objects, could very possibly be facts. The distances mentioned by [redacted] in his report are within a short distance of the actual distances on aeronautical charts of this area, although [redacted] has never consulted aeronautical charts of the type the Army uses. [redacted] stated that his business had suffered greatly since his report on July 25 due to the fact that at every stop on his business routes, large groups of people were waiting to question him as to just what he had seen. [redacted] stated further that if he, at any time in the future, saw anything in the sky, to quote [redacted] directly, "if I saw a ten story building

Part of Arnold's FBI File

from Chehalis, Washington, to Yakima, Washington, in his CallAir A-2 on a business trip. He made a brief detour after learning of a $5,000 reward for the discovery of a U.S. Marine Corps'C-46 transport airplane that had crashed near Mt. Rainier.The skies were completely clear and there was a mild wind.

Arnold would later recall, he saw a bright light—just a flash, like a glint of sun as it hits a mirror when the glass is angled just so. It had a blue-ish tinge. At first, he thought the light must have been coming from another plane; when he looked around, though, all he could see was a DC-4. It seemed to be flying about 15 miles away from him. It was not flashing. And then the lights came again—this time, in a series. Nine flashes, in rapid succession. Arnold originally described the objects' shape in many ways as: "flat like a pie pan", "shaped like a pie plate", and also described their erratic motion being "like a fish flipping in the sun" or a saucer skipped across water. From these, the press quickly coined the new terms "flying saucer" and "flying disc" to describe such objects, many of which were reported within days after Arnold's sighting. After his UFO sighting, Arnold became a minor celebrity, and for about a decade.

By the 1960s, Arnold had tired of his notoriety and UFOs in general, and he eventually declined all interviews. On June 24, 1977, however, he attended the First International UFO. Congress in Chicago, curated by Fate to mark the 30th anniversary of the "birth" of the modern UFO age. Some of his comments at the event reflected his displeasure at the general ignorance concerning the matter. Finally, the U.S. Air Force formally listed the Arnold's case as a mirage. However, before classified this incident as a "mirage", FBI agents questioned Kenneth Arnold.

The Maury Island Incident (June 21, 1947) refers to claims made by Fred Crisman and Harold Dahl of falling debris and threats by men in black following sightings of unidentified flying objects in the sky over Maury Island in Puget Sound Harold Dahl was on a conservation mission on the Puget Sound near the eastern shore of Washington's Maury Island, gathering logs, when he saw six donut-shaped obstacles hovering about a half a mile above his boat. Before long, one of them fell nearly 1,500 feet, followed by raining, metallic debris, some of which hit Dahl's son, Charles, on his arm, as well as the family dog, who didn't survive the ordeal. Dahl was able to take some pictures of the aircraft with his camera, which he later showed to his supervisor, Fred Crisman. A skeptical Crisman went back to the scene to look for himself and saw a strange aircraft with his own eyes. The following morning, Dahl was visited by a man in a black suit. They end up at a local diner, where the man was able to recount in extraordinary detail what Dahl had just experienced. "What I have said is proof to you that I know a great deal more about this experience of yours than you will want to believe," the man said, according to author Gray Barker's 1956 book: *They Knew Too Much About Flying Saucers*. Dahl was told not to speak of the incident. If he did, bad things would happen. The incident at Maury Island ignited the legend of the Men in Black.

In 1947, Harold Dahl claimed to have been warned not to talk about his alleged UFO sighting on Maury Island by a man in a dark suit. In the mid 1950s, the ufologist Will Smith claimed he was visited by men in dark suits who threatened and warned him not to continue investigating

UFOs. Albert Bender believed the men in black were secret government agents tasked with suppressing evidence of UFOs. The ufologist John Keel claimed to have had encounters with men in black and referred to them as "demonic supernaturals" with "dark skin and/or "exotic" facial features". According to the ufologist Jerome Clark, reports of men in black represent "experiences" that "don't seem to have occurred in the world of consensus reality.

The most celebrated MIB case was that reponed by UFO investigator and author Alben K. Bender. In July,1953 he was allegedly 'silenced' by three MIBs.These men are not a myth, nor a folklore, they are really FBI agents. Bender stated that all of them were dressed in black clothes. They looked like clergymen, but wore hats similar to Homburg style. The notorious Men In Black, always in threes, they made it clear to Bender that he was to cease all UFO work. Before departing the MIB confiscated copies of *Space Review,* and in their wake, a yellow mist appeared. And, once again, the odor of sulphur. Albert shut down the *International Flying Saucer Bureau*. The final issue of *Space Review* was released in October 1953 and included a cryptic warning: *We advise those engaged in saucer work to be very cautious.*

Albert K. Bender (June 16, 1921 – March 29, 2016), was an american author of the 1962 nonfiction book Flying Saucers and the Three Men, and a ufologist. He was obsessed with the UFO phenomenon and became a UFO researcher, founding the International Flying Saucers Bureau. In 1965, he founded the Max Steiner Music Society.

Bender was born on June 16, 1921 in Duryea, Pennsylvania. He lived with his stepfather. Bender worked as a factory clerk. He was drawn to the supernatural; he fashioned haunted house decorations and horror movie scenes on his walls. He attended high school in West Pittston, Pennsylvania. Bender was even featured in a newspaper article when he was 18 for writing to people all over the world. He wrote letters to correspondents in various countries including Peru, England, Romania, and Japan. These letters were up to 20 pages long. His goal was to collect things from different countries, like coins or sand, through writing his correspondences. During high school, he was also part of the American Youth League, and was elected the Jr. Vice President in January 1941, and was also elected national treasure in October of that same year.

Bender served in the United States Army Air Forces during World War II, from June 8, 1942-October 7, 1943. During this time, he visited Ottawa, Ontario, Canada for one week in August 1941. While in the Army, he was stationed at Fort George G. Meade as a dental technician and later transferred to Langley, Virginia. He worked there as a clerk for the Dental Center. He also became an editor for an Army newspaper in Langley. He later went to Bridgeport, Connecticut. After his honorable discharge from active service at Langley Field, Virginia, Bender relocated to Bridgeport with his mother Ellen and step-father Michael Ardolino. The family lived at 784 Broad Street. According to Bender, MIB arrived in Bridgeport during 1953. they appeared at his Broad Street home, just a few hundred yards from the main library.

Albert was employed as chief timekeeper at Acme Shear Co., the world's largest manufacturer of scissors. The factory was located across the Pequonnock River from downtown at Hicks and Knowlton Streets. Bender filled his living space with an assortment of twenty chiming clocks. Every fifteen minutes, half hour and on the hour, 784 Broad Street resounded with the din of bells. Seems that timekeeper enjoyed his privacy living in the attic (and its small connected den) of his step-father's three-story Broad Street home. At some point when Bender entered his late-20s, he adorned his living space with a collection of oddities: Faux skulls, shrunken heads, and his own original, outsider art. Have felt in love with ghost stories and horror movies, he claimed his blood flowed with ancestral witchcraft. Bender called his attic room: "Chamber of Horrors."

After believing to have experienced a supernatural encounter in 1953, he was married on October 18, 1954 to Betty Rose. She believed that she had also been visited by supernatural beings .

Due to the UFO flap in the American West during the late 1940s, prompting Bender to form one of America's nascent UFO organizations. In 1952 the Park City resident organized the International Flying Saucer Bureau. World War I flying ace, and CEO of Eastern Airlines, Eddie Rickenbacker became an honorary member. Albert Einstein declined the invitation. The Bureau's 600 worldwide members, with Bender as president, were dedicated to furthering the study of these mysterious craft. Its headquarters were located in Albert's Bridgeport home. One of the group's most enthusiastic members, Max Krengel, also worked as a timekeeper at Acme Shear; he served as IFSB vice president and assistant director. The IFSB reached out to members around the world through a quarterly journal, Space Review. The newsletter shared stories of UFO sightings and offered theories about the origins of these seemingly inexplicable objects. Although the organization was a success at first, he suddenly shut it down in 1953.

As soon as Bender started the IFSB, strange occurrences plagued him in Bridgeport. Ill health, strange phone calls, and telepathic messages hounded him. These events coincidently mirrored an outbreak of UFO sightings over southern Connecticut. In addition, Albert felt as if he was being watched. November 1952, at a local movie theater Bender realized a strange man with glowing eyes observing him; and while walking home along Main Street Albert was shadowed. On a separate occasion late one night on Broad Street Bender reported he was telepathically hypnotized and levitated. But the worst phenomenon was the sickening odor filling his attic. The stench of burning sulphur.

In his Broad Street home, Albert mixed his UFO research with mental telepathy.Bender prompted readers of Space Review with a strange request: memorize and silently recite, on a particular day and time, a form letter penned by Bender. His goal was to connect with Alien life via the simultaneous thought-projection of hundreds of IFSB members. World Contact Day has born, or as Bender, and the IFSB officially preferred, "C-Day," commenced at 6 o'clock in the evening (EST) on March 15, 1953. The telepathic message opened: *Calling occupants of interplanetary craft! Calling occupants of interplanetary craft that have been observing our planet EARTH. We of IFSB wish to make contact with you. We are your friends.* However,

Bender's message did not go over well. His rooms continued to fill with the smell of sulphur and he was telepathically ordered to cease delivering his message. A yellow mist gathered in the attic. Undeterred, Bender announced that the July issue of *Space Review* would hold a "startling revelation." It never appeared in print.

Bender later told that in March 1953 he had been approached by three men in black. These men visited him in his house and communicated with him telepathically. He received a metal disk from them and instruction. He reported that he felt like he was being transported. These men apparently shared insights into the nature of UFOs. These men shared the origin of UFOs with Bender. Afterwards he became ill and didn't eat for three days. As a result of the visitation, Bender felt encouraged to share what he had seen with other UFO investigators, but was refused. Bender suffered frequent headaches after the three men visited him and his co-workers reported that he seemed scared.

His experiences were recorded in: *They Knew Too Much about Flying Saucers* by Gray Barker, Bender's IFSB associate. After his this experience, he did not speak of the event for nine years. In 1962, Bender wrote: *Flying Saucers and the Three Men* to tell his own story. In the book, Bender recounts that the men in black were from another planet. After Barker published his book, Bender abandoned his quest into the supernatural and UFO research, departed Bridgeport and relocated to California to manage a motel. Albert Bender passed away, at the age of 94, on March 29, 2016.

During his life, Bender reported that he had a second supernatural encounter. He was visited by three shadowy figures. They did not touch the floor, but hovered above it. They told him that their human appearance was an illusion and that whatever information he told people about their visitation would not be believed. They supposedly told him that they captured people from Earth and used their bodies to disguise themselves.

SPACE REVIEW was the official magazine about ufology news at that time in 1953. Late in the summer of 1953, Bender made a series of discoveries, which led him to believe that he had finally found the truth to the UFO cover-up. He had planned to reveal his findings in the next issue of *Space Review*, but before the issue was published, Bender was visited by three "men dressed in black," who had already read the unpublished report and confirmed his findings. The *silencers* as he called them, scared Bender to the point where he did not publish the report, but left a warning: Then, Bender shutdown his publication and dissolved the IFSB.

Like an omen from the Men in Black, Bender's home at 784 Broad Street no longer stands. This home where Alien communication from outer space, and mysterious Men in Black made their presence is no longer there due to a different invasion. Urban renewal. Bender's home suddenly vanishes. The federally constructed, Connecticut Thruway claimed Albert's residence. In addition, the State Street Redevelopment Project (1962-1968) razed practically everything, except the Bridgeport Public Library building. Finally, in 1967, the Southern Connecticut Gas Company's parking lot absorbed the former backyard of the "Chamber of Horrors." As a result,

SAC, New York   January 9, 1953

                    Director, FBI   28258

RECORD   18 RAY PALMER, EDITOR
              "OTHER WORLDS"
      105   INFORMATION CONCERNING (INTERNAL SECURITY)

            Attached for your information are two copies of a
letter forwarded to the Bureau by Mr. Walter Winchell, the
contents of which are self-explanatory.

            Bureau files reflect no identifiable information
relating to Ray Palmer or the publication "Other Worlds."

            Although the location of Palmer and the publication
of which he is the editor is not reflected in the incoming
communication, this data is being forwarded in the event
either Ray Palmer or the publication "Other Worlds" comes
to the attention of your office.

            You should search the files of your office for
any pertinent data concerning Ray Palmer or the publication
"Other Worlds" and thereafter be guided by current Bureau
instructions regarding the handling of security investigations.

Enclosure

NOTE ON YELLOW ONLY:

            Records maintained by Publication Desk and Bureau
Library fail to reflect any information concerning Ray Palmer
or the publication "Other Worlds."

MJM:jdt

Tolson ___
Ladd ___
Nichols ___
Belmont ___
Clegg ___
Glavin ___
Harbo ___
Rosen ___
Tracy ___
Laughlin ___
Mohr ___
Tele. ___
Holloman ___
Gandy ___

COMM — FBI
JAN 9 — 1953
MAILED 27

JAN 22 1953

ALL INFORMATION CONTAINED
HEREIN IS UNCLASSIFIED
DATE 5/14/80 BY SP-16SK/dg

W. C. Sullivan (in Books)

Part of Palmer's FBI File

Office Memorandum • UNITED STATES GOVERNMENT

TO : SAC, Detroit (65-2677)　　　　　　　DATE: 8-19-54

FROM : SA Charles W. Gregory

SUBJECT: GEORGE ADAMSKI, et al
ESPIONAGE

ALL INFORMATION CONTAINED
HEREIN IS UNCLASSIFIED
DATE 5/3/85 BY

On Aug. 19, 1954, MRS. LOUISE MOONEY, 8854 Stoepel, Detroit, contacted the writer and furnished a letter she had received captioned "Detroit Flying Saucer Club". MRS. MOONEY advised that she was going to attend the meeting of the club scheduled for 8-19-54 at the Veterans' Memorial Bldg, Detroit, and that she would report on the meeting and furnish any available literature given out at the meeting. She said that she had had no contact with the organization since she last contacted this office.

65- 2677-910

SEARCHED________INDEXED________
SERIALIZED________FILED________
AUG 20 1954
FBI - DETROIT

Part of Adamski's FBI File

Bender's portal to his Multiple Realities was forever closed. Conspiracy-minded readers wonders if this was just a coincidence that the government bulldozed his residence. As a result, all evidence of the MIB and Bender were eliminated from the Bridgeport streets scene.

However, MIB were not limited to the Bender Mystery. Seems that the FBI made an special unit that could be called MIB. The went behind the Shaver Mystery. Years back, the FBI destroyed Richard Shaver's FBI File according to the respond given to us under FOIA request. However, they did not destroyed Ray Palmer's FBI File. On December 24, 1952, the FBI took a closer look to Ray Palmer whereabouts. The reason for these Men in Black to move on Palmer was a handwritten letter, dated on December 15, 1952, received by Walter Winchell. Winchell forwarded it to the FBI, and the agency processed on January 9, 1953. In this letter, the writer (name and signature has been blocked out) accused Palmer of widespread "Commie Propaganda". The anonymous writer mentioned two stories written by Palmer in *Amazing Stories* (January, 1953): *Frontiers Beyond the Sun*, and *Death Beyond the Beil* as proof of the "Commie propaganda" made by Palmer .Also, FBI's MIB approached George Adamski about the same concern in the 50's.

Finally, for believers, Men in Black are real. For non believers, these men are fictional characters. However, it is undeniable that some sort of secret agents from the US Goverment have questioned people that had experienced the UFO phenomena. Because the government considered them a threat to national security.

ALFRED K. BENDER'S PHOTOS

Bender's Attic Room

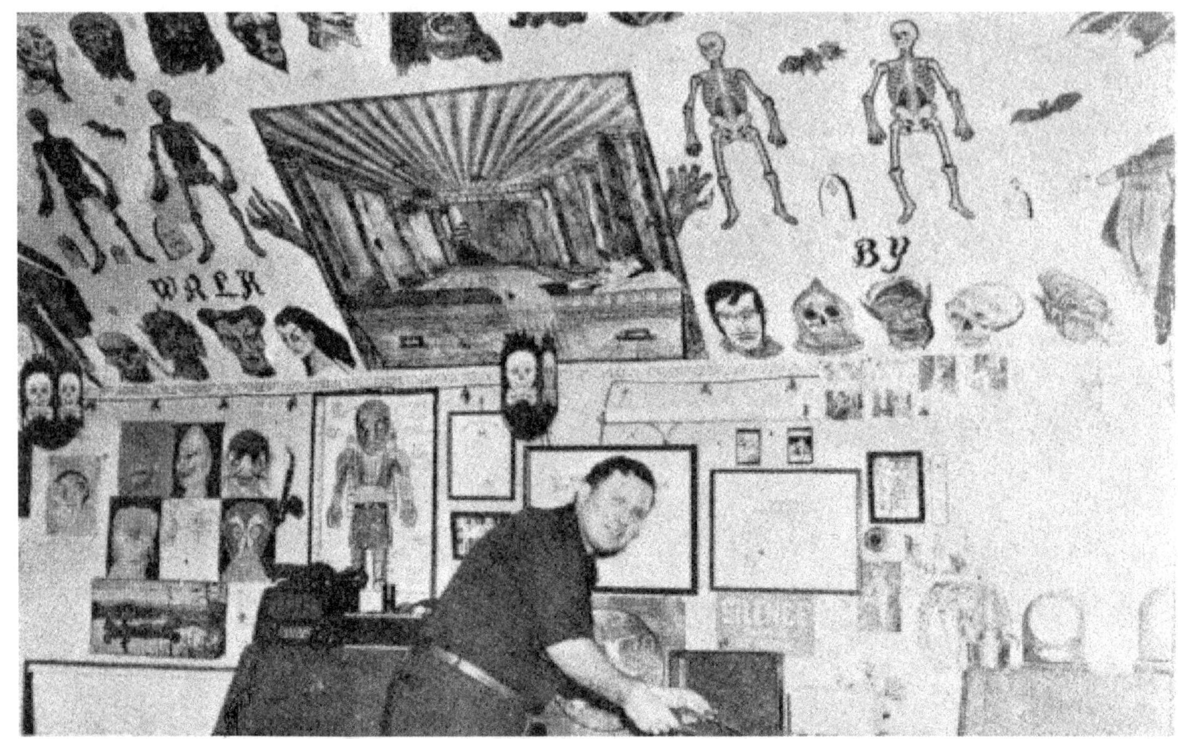

Bender's Attic Room "Chamber of Horrors"

Bender's Attic Room "Chamber of Horrors"

Albert K Bender as a young man

Albert K Bender military portrait WW II

Albert K Bender sitting

Albert K Bender and his father

Albert K Bender and Wife

Albert K. Bender's Sketch of Men in Black

Albert K. Bender's Portrait of Men in Black

ALFRED K. BENDER'S DOCUMENTS

REGISTRATION CARD—(Men born on or after February 17, 1897 and on or before December 31, 1921)

SERIAL NUMBER	1. NAME (Print)	ORDER NUMBER
T 1400	Albert (First) Kenneth (Middle) Bender (Last)	T 10050

2. PLACE OF RESIDENCE (Print)

226 Fremont St W. Pittston Luz. Pa.
(Number and street) (Town, township, village, or city) (County) (State)

[THE PLACE OF RESIDENCE GIVEN ON THE LINE ABOVE WILL DETERMINE LOCAL BOARD JURISDICTION; LINE 2 OF REGISTRATION CERTIFICATE WILL BE IDENTICAL]

3. MAILING ADDRESS

Same
[Mailing address if other than place indicated on line 2. If same insert word same]

4. TELEPHONE	5. AGE IN YEARS	6. PLACE OF BIRTH
No	20	Duryea (Town or county)
(Exchange) (Number)	DATE OF BIRTH June 16 1921 (Mo.) (Day) (Yr.)	Pa. (State or country)

7. NAME AND ADDRESS OF PERSON WHO WILL ALWAYS KNOW YOUR ADDRESS

Mrs Fred Herron 226 Fremont St W. Pittston Pa.

8. EMPLOYER'S NAME AND ADDRESS

Dept. of Health Kirby Health Center

9. PLACE OF EMPLOYMENT OR BUSINESS

71 N. Franklin St. Wilkes Barre Luz. Pa.
(Number and street or R. F. D. number) (Town) (County) (State)

I AFFIRM THAT I HAVE VERIFIED ABOVE ANSWERS AND THAT THEY ARE TRUE.

Albert Kenneth Bender

D. S. S. Form 1 (Revised 1-1-42) (over) ☆ GPO 16—21630-1 (Registrant's signature)

Albert Kenneth Bender
in the U.S., World War II Draft Cards Young Men, 1940-1947

Name:	Albert Kenneth Bender
Age:	20
Relationship to Draftee:	Self (Head)
Birth Date:	16 Jun 1921
Birth Place:	Duryea, Pennsylvania, USA
Residence Place:	West Pittston, Luzerne, Pennsylvania, USA
Registration Date:	16 Feb 1942
Registration Place:	West Pittston, Luzerne, Pennsylvania, USA
Employer:	Kirby Health Center
Weight:	167
Complexion:	Ruddy
Eye Color:	Blue
Hair Color:	Brown
Height:	5 10
Next of Kin:	Fred Herron

Form No. 1

COMMONWEALTH OF PENNSYLVANIA
WORLD WAR II VETERANS' COMPENSATION BUREAU

APPLICATION FOR WORLD WAR II COMPENSATION—TO BE USED BY HONORABLY DISCHARGED VETERAN OR PERSON STILL IN SERVICE

IMPORTANT—Before Filling Out This Form Study it Carefully.

Read and Follow Instructions—Print Plainly in Ink or Use Typewriter. DO NOT Use Pencil—All Signatures Must Be in Ink.

Applicant Must Not Write In Space Below

APR 1 1950
Date Application Was Received

Batch Control Number
64698 11380

1—Name of Applicant.

BENDER (Last)   ALBERT (First)   K. (Middle or Initial)

2—Address to Which CHECK and MAIL is to be Sent.

784 BROAD ST. (House No. St. R. D. P. O. Box)   BRIDGEPORT 4 (City or Town)   (County)   CONN. (State)

Active Domestic Service
Months 16 $ 160
Days $
Amount Due $

3—Date and Place of Birth.

6 (Month)   16 (Day)   21 (Year)   Duryea (City or Town)   Luzerne (County)   Penna (State)

4—Name Under Which Applicant Served In World War II.

BENDER (Last)   ALBERT (First)   K (Middle or Initial)

Active Foreign Service
Months 0 $
Days $
Amount Due $

5—Date of Beginning and Date of Ending of Each Period of Service Between December 7, 1941 and March 2, 1946 (Both Dates Inclusive) During Which Applicant Was In DOMESTIC SERVICE.

June 8, 1942 —————— Oct. 7, 1943
Date of Beginning   Date of Ending

Total Amt. Due $ 160

Audited By

Service Computed By

6—Date of Beginning and Date of Ending of Each Period of Service Between December 7, 1941 and March 2, 1946 (Both Dates Inclusive) During Which Applicant Was In FOREIGN SERVICE.

—— NONE ——

Date of Beginning   Date of Ending

Amounts Extended By

Approved For Payment
Date OCT 1950
For A. G.
For Aud. G.
For S. T.
Application Disapproved
By

7—Date and Place Applicant Entered Active Service.

June 8, 1942 (Month Day Year)   Wilkes-Barre, Pa. (Place)

8—Service or Serial Numbers Assigned To Applicant.

Service No's.

Serial No's. 33345715

9—Date and Place Where Applicant Was Separated From Active Service.

October 7, 1943 (Month Day Year)   Langley Field, Virginia. (Place)

10—Is Applicant Now Serving In Armed Forces On Active Duty?   Yes ________   No X

If Answer is YES—Be Sure To Have Certificate Executed And Filed With Application—See Instruction Sheet.

11—Mark "X" Above Name To Indicate Sex And Branch of Service.

X Male   Female   X Army   Navy   Marine Corps   Coast Guard   Other—Describe

12—Applicant's Residence At Time of Entry Into Active Service.

226 (House No.)   Fremont (Street)   (R. D.)   (P. O. Box)   West Pittston (City or Town)   Luzerne (County)   Penna (State)

13—Applicant Was Registered Under Selective Service As Follows.

#1 (Draft Board No.)   Wyoming (City or Town)   Luzerne (County)   Penna. (State)

ALFRED K. BENDER'S NEWSPAPER ARTICLES

Don't Be Afraid, Darling; It's Bender

By ETHEL BECKWITH

dents. Once I took some bodies out of the water, it gave me a real and thunder rolling from a phonograph record.

By ETHEL BECKWITH

Albert Bender doesn't look like a creep, but you should see his room at 784 Broad St.

"My Chamber of Horrors," he calls it joyously.

Dead faces in their coffins, skeletons, skulls, blood-drooling vampires and other cute fugitives from Inner Sanctum, stare and glare at Bender from every corner. He painted them and he's glad.

Not satisfied with visual horror, Bender has worked out sound effects for thunder, sobbings and hissings. Lying down in this room nights, Bender is as happy as the Charles Addam characters in The New Yorker — they love their picture window because it faces a graveyard.

The Herald visitor was one of the first Bender has admitted through his chamber door. It was in the light of a privilege. After all, he spends all his offtime here and he doesn't care for people who might faint away. What he enjoys is the look of iced horror.

Bender is chief timekeeper at the Acme Shear Co. Nights he helps his stepfather, M. A. Ardoline, fix supper and as soon as possible he vanishes out of this world.

He says he learned to paint through correspondence schools after going to high school in West Pittston, Pa. Came from Pennsyl-

vania about eight years ago, mother died after leaving him a supply of skull cutouts which she sewed at his request.

These cloth skulls Bender has sewed on his black—of course—drapery around a dreary-viewed window.

"She thought the little man in white would be after me," Bender recalled his mother. "But I always liked the supernatural and the weird. I have some American Indian blood in me. 'Way back," he exulted, "there was witchcraft in my family."

(The reporter took a quick look: Bender has the regular five-fingered hand, while to be an Addams creep, you have six fingers.)

"When I was in the Air Force down in Virginia," Bender went on' "I saw some real gruesome acci-

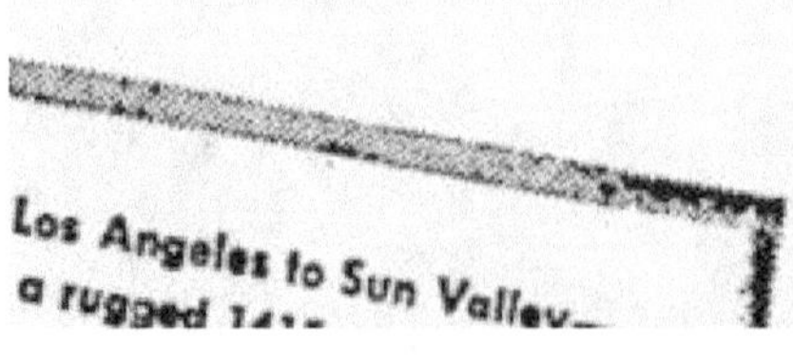

xxiv

dents. Once I took some bodies out of the water—it gave me a real kick," he said with a quiet rapture.

DARK LAUGHTER

Always trying to perfect his sanctum, the daring fellow also has things fixed so that certain luminous lights produce the effect of abandon-all-hope to the point of having clouds expand and contract sensuously over the "sky," and thunder rolling from a phonograph record.

Showing how tireless he is, Bender also writes spook plays and records his own thoughts, which he sends around the country in what he calls "telespondence."

He has a brother Fred in town, and a sister Mrs. Shirley Audugar. In Albany is another sister, Mrs. Joseph Kevlin.

SOLVED FLYING SAUCER RIDDLE . . . But Albert K. Bender, above, Bridgeport science enthusiast, abandoned further research of flying saucers after being visited by three mysterious men in black. Bender doesn't frighten easily, as indicated by one of his macabre bedroom ornaments.

ALFRED K. BENDER'S FBI FILE

DEPARTMENT OF CIVIL DEFENSE

MONROE AND JACKSON STREETS
FRANKLIN, INDIANA

ROBERT D. WOLF
Director

20 January 1953

Mr. J. Edgar Hoover
Director Federal Bureau of Investigation
Washington, D. C.

Dear Sir:

I would first like to apologize for writing to you direct, however, I have cleared this morning with our State Director and he suggests this procedure.

We have been having some success with our Ground Observation Corps as we have four (4) posts here in the county.

Last Fall I was contacted by one of our local business men wanting to know if I would be interested in joining the International Flying Saucer Bureau. I told him that I would and did join with the idea fully in mind of having the local people who are interested in Flying Saucers also work in our Civil Defense Program. We are only too willing to co-operate in any way we can with Civil Defense. The city of Franklin is approximately twenty (20) miles southwest of Indianapolis, on the dual lane highway U S #31.

I am enclosing a letter which was received last October, as well as the current issue of SPACE REVIEW. Would like to know if this organization has been cleared or is subversive in any way.

I would appreciate your expediting this information back to us so that we will know what steps to take in further enlisting interested persons in our program.

If you do not require the enclosures please return them.

ROBERT D. WOLF

Home Address:
19 North Forsythe St.
Franklin, Indiana.

RECORDED-84

INDEXED-84

2

EXCERPTS FROM A SUMMARY OF A FIVE-YEAR FLYING SAUCER INVESTIGATION

By George D. Fawcett, International Council, IFSB

I have just decided to stop investigation that I began a little over five years ago on one of the most fascinating mysteries of modern times, that being the well known "Flying Saucer" phenomena. Since the summer of 1947 when the first saucer scare broke out in the United States, I have spent much of my time, money and energy seeking a solution to this riddle. While carrying on my private investigations I was able to interview several astronomers, scientists, pilots and guided missile experts, who had spotted these saucers or who had been investigating or studying these strange objects. In addition to these I have talked to many eye-witnesses who had sighted these objects throughout the United States and have mailed questionnaires out to many others.

I have kept bulletins and scrapbooks on the saucers for the past five years, and while doing this I wrote a six-page pamphlet entitled "The Flying Saucer Phenomena" for my teachers, and classmates I have lectured to several groups in Lynchburg. I have been interested in this phenomena from the very first, my sighting of an orange-red globe which hovered for four minutes over the Lynchburg College administration building in Lynchburg, Virginia, on the morning of July 6, 1951, has increased my interest threefold since then. This is one of my reasons for stopping my investigation. It's really too big a job for one person to handle. We must realize that we are dealing with a phenomena that is as fantastic as it is fascinating. Many of the reports that I was able to gather in my collection tend to back this statement.

Some recent thoughts about the "flying saucers" are that perhaps there will be some landings soon. This doesn't seem too far fetched, that these flying saucers are still being seen everywhere, for longer periods and in groups instead of alone, as well as more reports of huge saucer or rocket ships. Then, too, they seem to come and go at will, perhaps being stationed as satellites themselves.

I feel that our government must know something about these saucers because in my opinion at this very moment the United States Government is carrying on an educational program regarding interplanetary travel in our country. Perhaps space ships from other planets are already here! At any rate, whether they are trying to prevent religious controversy or panic or for any other reasons which they might have, our government is still releasing, denying, suppressing and investigating reports and materials for some reason.

Regardless, the future will tell! In closing, I'd like to use a favorite phrase of Charlie Berry, Lynchburg College student who said, "things are really looking up." I wonder if things aren't looking DOWN, too; Sooner or later we're bound to find out, and all I can say is, "the sooner, the better."

EDITOR'S NOTE: Mr. Fawcett's discussions and opinions will be found in future issues of Space Review.

ATTENTION MEMBERS AND OFFIC... would be interested in receiving emblem to wear on your coat lapel with... your club letters "IFSB" engraved on a background, we would be interested in... wing. We could order these emblems if we get enough people showing interest... approximately $1.00 Please let us know as soon as possible. T... you

WE WANT YOU TO MEET

EDGAR L. PLUNKETT, BRITISH REPRESENTATIVE—Born at Bristol, Glos., England, on December 26, 1903. Covered most parts of the world as a radio operator at sea from 1922 to 1936, including the U. S., notably New York, Boston, Baltimore, Norfolk, Newport News, Tampa, Mobile and many other ports. Has many interesting memories of the prohibition days, the gangster era, Jack Dempsey, Babe Ruth, Lou Gehrig and other notable highlights. Has worked for many years for Anglo-American friendship and still corresponds with friends here in U.S.A. Was called to service in 1939. Was rescued from Dunkirk Beaches by the French Destroyer L'Incomprise on June 1, 1940. Went to Middle East in 1941, and served through three Western Desert Campaigns with the British 8th Army. After fall of Tunis was commissioned in Palestine and was then posted in Egypt. Returned to England at the end of the war after four and a half years service overseas as a Captain. Now employed by his original firm as a clerk.

He has a wife and three children, the ages are Denis 21, now with the RAF, Diana 18, and Michael 14. Hobbies are writing and reading and other journalistic yearnings including poetry, plus an unabated desire to travel. Since the formation of Civil Defense a year or so ago, he has become a qualified instructor and lectures three evenings weekly to industrial personnel.

Mr. Plunkett has shown great interest in IFSB activities and will without a doubt prove to be our most valuable foreign representative.

ASSOCIATE EDITOR

(Next Issue April 1, 1953)

POST OFFICE BOX 241

BRIDGEPORT 2, CONN.

U.S.A.

Return Postage Guaranteed

To

Mr. Robert D. Wolf
19 N. Forsyth St.
Franklin, Indiana
10155

SAUCER SIGHTINGS BY IFSB MEMBERS

Exclusive! From Franklin, Indiana and Surrounding Towns

SIGHTING NO. 4—On the morning of July 28, 1952 in the skies to the southeast and at times directly over Franklin, Indiana appeared three strange objects. Their flight was watched by a large number of men of sound mind and character. The following is compiled from a Police report turned in by Capt. Ice Sloan, Patrolman Jack W. Moore and Patrolman Kenneth Rund of the Franklin, Indiana Police Department on Monday morning, July 28, 1952 at 6:00 a.m. These objects were witnessed by policemen, civilian authorities, and members of the United States Army. After notifying all proper authorities of the objects no definite steps were taken by the army or otherwise. The report is as follows:

There were three objects, one larger ... ghter than the two smaller objects. The larger of the three seemed to cast off a w... ...lowish light. Its pattern of flight seemed to be that of a circle. It seemed to alwa... ...keeping track of the two smaller objects. The two smaller objects cast off a distinct ...light of their own, one being an orange hue and the other a reddish color. The two s... ...ones seemed to be in a dog fight all their ow... since they executed barrel rolls, loops ...and spins. They made turns of 90 degrees and 45 degrees without losing any ... of ...ed, as well as dancing up and down as if someone was playing with a giant yo-yo. The objects made single sorties to the south completely out of sight, to return almost immediately into view again, joining the other in a neat... ...show of turns, loops and spins. We estimated their height at approximately 1... while their speed varied from an estimated 1500 miles per hour to an estimated ... ...s per hour. Even with a pair of binoculars it was almost an impossibility ... any exact shape other than that they appeared to be round and flat as a sa... ...y were observed for a period of four hours and fifteen minutes. Dawn came at ... a.m. and all stars had gone around 5:00 a.m. At 5:03 a.m. it was bright daylight—and the three objects were still visible. Their color did not change in daylight. At 5:11 a.m. the larger of the three objects was joined by the two smaller ones; the smaller objects one at a time disappeared ...the larger, first the orange, then the red. After ...to envelope the two smaller objects it moved ...and to the west out of sight. The ...the three objects and the ...appearance of the larger took exactly 40 seconds. ...cts were verified by: E... ...Police Dept., Camp Atterbury, Ind.; Columbus ...pt.; Seymour State Police P... Greensburg Police Dept., North Vernon Police ...Connersville ... Dept ...ville State Police Post, Fort Wayne, Ind.; and ...son, Ind. Mr. ... and M... ...Rund are IFSB members now.

...ntative for Minnesota

...airie, Minnesota about 2:30 p.m., April ...250 MPH and when it ascended their ...was visable for about 45 seconds. Direc-...path.

SIGHTING NO. 6—Alan K. S... ...m ...California

Sighted a disc shaped object ...e East of Los Angeles about 9:08 p.m. on September 22, 1952. It was a yellow ...ite in color, and remained in a stationary position for about 4 seconds. It was al... ...grees about the horizon. It was about 50 feet in diameter and traveling due so...

...sending in ... Sightings, please give the date that you ...Tempt you?

TO ALL MEMBERS OF THE I.F.S.B.—
GREETINGS FROM ENGLAND
Capt. Edgar L. Plunkett, British Representative

Are we on the verge of a breath-taking discovery? Yes, I believe we really are! To quote Captain Eddie Rickenbacker, "Too many good men have seen Flying Saucers for us to dismiss them lightly as hallucinations."

The nineteenth and twentieth centuries have produced a number of astonishing discoveries notably the dreaded atom bomb, and also has had to discard in many cases previously held convictions such as that "matter is indestructible".

Even the average layman today, due to increased educational facilities, and access to literature of all kinds, has a very good idea that life in all its forms consists of "energy", and that this energy somehow links back to some form of pulsating orbital structure like unto the universe, but on an infinitesimally small scale. Therefore, it is—to me at least—quite believable that it is possible that somewhere—something—someone—has solved the riddle of this energy, etheric, electromagnetic, call it what you will. Having progressed so far, it follows that given elements capable of withstanding immense stresses and strains, a propulsion of what has become known as the "Flying Saucer" becomes a possibility. It is known that between the Sun, Moon, and our Earth, and presumably between other inter planetary and possibly interstellar bodies there exists magnetic lines of force, thus if some form of aircraft or saucer has control of the means of attraction and repulsion, these lines of force which by the way never touch one another, would form the perfect highway along which to travel at the speed of light, and probably very much faster. It would also account for the capability of these so-called "saucers" to accomplish right-angled turns, inasmuch that these known magnetic waves emanate in all directions. Therefore, from the point of view of the average thinking man in the street, I say, "I believe the flying saucer does exist, and that the coming years will vindicate such men as Captain Mantell, Kenneth Arnold, and countless other pioneers in this field." In conclusion, may I say to all IFSB members at home and abroad, "carry on the good work, and above all, do not be disappointed, discouraged or blinded by the jeers and sneers of the ignorant so-called majority."

The best of everything for the New Year ahead!

Your faithfully,   E. L. PLUNKETT

MYSTERIOUS CRAFT
by Gail Sprague

Out of the dark, mysterious, depths of
   space,
Came strange looking craft at a tremendous pace.
Their course was true, the third planet
   from the sun,
Their orders: Don't return until your task
   is done.
Down they descended; some got out.
"Be back in 24 hours," the commander
   told the scout.
Time went fast, all returned.
Off went the craft, bearing all they'd
   learned.
The decision was reached, never again,
On this small planet they'd ever land.
Wars, corruption, prejudice and greed,
Made this the worst of all planets, all
   agreed

OUT THERE
by Victor Root

Out in space lies my destiny,
Out there, beyond the clouds;
Where winds have not yet blown,
Where man has not yet gone;
That's where I long to roam.

Out in space lies my destiny,
Out there, among the stars;
Where night is forever ruling,
Where solitude is soothing;
That's where I long to roam.

Give me a silver ship,
To make a happy trip,
Out there, among the stars.

DIRECTORY OF REPRESENTATIVES

The following are additional representatives since our last publication.

BRITISH REPRESENTATIVE—Edgar L. Plunkett, 71 Chedworth Rd., Horfield, Bristol 7, England; Assistant Representative for Britain- -Denis Plunkett

PUERTO RICAN REPRESENTATIVE—Luis Luhring, Box 23, Punta Santiago

COLORADO—Verna M. Hampton, 4245 Alcott St., Denver

MAINE—Allan Levinsky, 59 Atlantic St., Portland

MISSOURI—Ralph Hetzel, 6 Scarsdale, St. Louis 17

NEW JERSEY—August C. Roberts, 443 Ogden Ave., Jersey City

NORTH CAROLINA—David T. Benton, Box 430, E.C.C., Greenville

OHIO—Robert C. Schnelle, Sr., 714 McMann Ave., Cincinnati

OREGON—G. L. McColly, 524 Jersey St., Beaverton

DISTRICT OF COLUMBIA—Rev. S. L. Daw, 5119—7th St., N.W., Washington

WEST VIRGINIA—Gray Barker, Box 981, Clarksburg

Above names will not be published again. Additional names in future issues.

Anyone that wishes to correspond with other members will please send us permission to print your name and address so that others will know that you desire correspondence. We do not publish lists of our members names and addresses without permission from them.

LET'S LOOK AT THE MAGAZINES

READERS DIGEST FOR JULY——Two articles "Have We Visitors from Space," and "Flying Saucers—New in Name Only."

TRUE MAGAZINE, SEPT. 1952—"The Flying Saucers and the Mysterious Little Men." OCT. 1952—"We Flew Above Flying Saucers." NOV. 1952—"What Radar Tells About Flying Saucers."

COLLIER'S MAGAZINE, OCT. 20, 1952—"Moonbound," Page 18.

COLLIER'S, OCT. 18, 1952—"Man on the Moon." OCT. 25, 1952—"More About Man on the Moon."

PIC MAGAZINE, NOV. 1952—"How Do Saucers Fly?"

SIR MAGAZINE, DEC. 1952—"Flying Saucers and the Air Around Us."

MR. MAGAZINE, JAN. 1953—"Is Washington Afraid of Flying Saucers?"

MAN TO MAN MAGAZINE, JAN. 1953—"Flying Saucers Are Not New."

THE MYSTERY OF OTHER WORLDS REVEALED—A Fawcett Book No. 166. Excellent! A four star edition—one of the finest to date in the pulp line. Cost 75c. We advise all saucer-minded folks to get this magazine. It is only once in a great while the publisher puts out such fine publication. Contains news of Space Travel; Flying Saucers; and Rocket Development.

These magazines are in the L.A.G.R.S. LIBRARY as part of our collection. We will send written information to anyone who have questions on above magazines.

Coming in April "SPACE REVIEW"—"SAUCERITIS" by John Armitage of England. An article that will make you really THINK!

A COMPLETE LISTING OF ALL OF OUR OFFICERS AND COUNCIL MEMBERS

HIGHLIGHTS ABOUT REPRESENTATIVES

DICK CAMPBELL, Rep. Indiana—Rep. Campbell has written us many interesting letters and aided in making his home town of Franklin the only city in the world with the most IFSB members. At present it totals over twenty. He was assisted by Mr. Louis Frahm, and Mr. Jack Moore of that place.

* * *

J. RONALD ALBERT, rep. Ontario, Canada—Will be appointed Representative of CANADA AT LARGE. Doing a fine job. Would like more Canadians to join club.

* * *

VICTOR ROOT, Rep. Illinois—One of our most valuable representatives. He has spent much time preparing a map of the United States showing the places where saucers have been seen. He is quite a poet, too; see his poem in this issue. Mr. Root presented the IFSB with his saucer map. We are proud of it. We are sorry to say that Mr. Root may have to move to California in the near future. It will be very hard to replace such an ardent worker.

* * *

HARRY BROADDUS, Rep. Kentucky—Obtained two new members for IFSB. One of them, Mrs. Glenn C. Fuller, saw a flying saucer. Her report will be in our next issue of "Space Review". Mr. Broaddus is spreading the word about IFSB.

* * *

DIANE BUCHANAN, Rep. Iowa—Obtained a new member, and has clippings she intends to send in to IFSB.

* * *

GAIL SPRAGUE, Rep. Wisconsin—Gail is quite the cartoonist. She sent in a cartoon that really made the International Staff roll off their chairs. She showed the parlor of a home with the front door open, a strange looking creature had walked in the door leaving muddy tracks on the floor. Outside can be seen a saucer parked on the lawn. A housewife approaches the creature and this is what she says: "I don't care where you're from. Look at my clean rug.'" She also sent us a fine poem that appears in this issue. Gail obtained a new member for us also. She sure is showing fine interest.

* * *

ALLAN LEVINSKY, Rep. Maine—Claims that very few people are seeing saucers in Maine. Is doing his best to get people interested in IFSB.

* * *

ROBERT R. RITTER, Rep. Tennessee—Chalks up another member for IFSB.

* * *

LUIS LUHRING, Rep. Puerto Rico—Mr. Luhring has sent us numerous clippings from Puerto Rico about saucers. He plans to get as many people as possible to join IFSB. He says that the interest in saucers is as great in Puerto Rico as anyplace else.

* * *

S. L. DAW, Rep. Washington, D.C.—We are happy to have for our representative in Washington, D.C., the first member of the clergy, Reverend Daw. Mr. Daw, as he prefers to be called by club members, is doing great work for IFSB. We are anxiously awaiting to see his actual photos of saucers, that he took himself.

* * *

RONALD KINNEAR, Rep. New York—Took upon himself to advertise in his own state and had 50 post cards printed and plans to mail them out, in his state.

* * *

We are not getting any reports from some of our Representatives. It is absolutely necessary that we hear from you, so please do your best to get those monthly reports rolling in on time.

"MY THEORY"
by IFSB Members

THEORY NO. 6—Submitted by BARBARA KNORR, Member from Connecticut

Everybody seems to believe that the "saucers", whatever they are, come from this Solar System. I do not believe any other planet but ours can support intelligent life. Perhaps plant life, but not human.

I do believe that if our planet can support life, why not other planets in other Solar Systems. I do not believe that these people wish to destroy us because if they had they could have done so long ago. Also, how do we know that these things we see are not beings themselves.

THEORY NO. 7—Submitted by Representative LOUIE MASONICK, JR., of Minnesota

My theory is one most IFSB members seem to have. First, I believe they are from another planet. All those stars must have something going around them. All those celestial bodies must be up there for some reason, besides to look at. Then, also, they may even be from our Solar System.

I do not think an official agency of our government should come out and say—"we do not know what they are and whether or not they are a menace." The best way to reveal the objects would be through clubs like the IFSB. I do not believe that they are a menace. I think there is intelligent life on them and that they are just observing us.

THEORY NO. 8—Submitted by Representative ALAN RIEVMAN of Connecticut

My theory on the origin of the "flying saucers" is that they are definitely real and are from one of the planets of our Solar System. I do not believe that they are from one of the other Solar Systems. These "neighbors" probably thought that our planet could not have intelligent life upon it, but with the last atomic explosion they may have changed their minds.

... n sure that they are not from Earth because if they were ours it would be impossible ... p it quiet and if they were from a foreign government they wouldn't be flying over ... ited States. They would risk being shot down and their secret revealed to us.

THEORY NO. 9—Submitted by Representative VICTOR ROOT of Illinois

My theory is that the "flying saucers" are manned ships controlled and operated by intelligent creatures who are scouting our world. They will not try to make contact with us for many reasons. One is that we are too warlike and emotional. Another is that we have diseases which may harm or even kill them. Some day when we reach out and touch the planets we may meet them. A race of intelligent creatures other than ourselves, certainly does exist.

THEORY NO. 10—Submitted by ALAN STAZER, Member from California

I think that the "flying saucers" are from the solar system of ALPHA or PROXIMA CENTUARI. Most likely the 3rd or 4th planet. The planet is probably about 4000 miles in diameter and two-thirds as big as the earth. Some other reasons are that Centauri is too far distant for observation of such a small body as a planet. This star is of about the same size and the same spectral, type-GO, as the Sun. Editor's Note: WOW!

All theories become the property of IFSB and cannot be returned.

SCIENCE FICTION NEWS

Alan C. Rievman

Victor Root, Illinois Rep. of IFSB, has some Science-Fiction mags for sale, or free in exchange. He is selling them for a small fee. Write to IFSB for address.

The DECEMBER, 1952, issue of FATE magazine is a must to all IFSB members and officers. It contains an article by Curtis Fuller, entitled, "Let's Get Straight About the Saucers." A complete detailed story of the incident of the scoutmaster described in our January issue, is discussed with a picture of the scoutmaster. SUBSCRIBE TO FATE MAGAZINE AND KEEP UP TO DATE ON THE SAUCERS. Write to 806 Dempster Street, Evanston, Illinois.

New Pocket Books on Stands: Dell No. 627, "When Worlds Collide" by Philip Wylie and Edwin Balmer. Pocket Book No. 903, "New Tales of Space and Time", edited by Raymond J. Healy.

Thanks to Ray Palmer for our letter in the December issue of "Other Worlds" Clark Publishing Co., 806 Dempster St., Evanston, Illinois. Let's subscribe.

NEW BOOK BY VIKING PRESS "Across the Space Frontier", edited by Cornelius Ryan, $3.95, Viking, New York.

RANDOM HOUSE HAS DONE IT AGAIN WITH: "By Space Ship to the Moon", written by Jack Coggins and Fletcher Pratt, foreword by Willy Ley. $1.

SCIENCE FICTION NEWS-LETTER, by our Council Member, "Bob" Tucker, P.O. Box 702, Bloomington, Illinois.

THE UNITED STATES ROCKET SOCIETY, Box 29, Glen Ellyn, Illinois.

Hollywood is coming out with two good movies: "War of the Worlds" and "The Conquest of Space".

SAUCER REVIEW, by Elliott Rockmore, a member of our Council. P.O. Box 118, Wall St. Station, New York 5, N.Y.

Owners of tape recorders or wire recorders Join T.R.I. (Tape-respondence International. Send your voice to your correspondents) 3488—22nd St., San Francisco 10, Calif.

BORDERLAND SCIENCES RESEARCH ASSOCIATES located at 3524 Adams Ave., San Diego 16, California, would like to have IFSB members join their society.

Many new Science Fiction Mags are hitting the newsstands and some are good while others are the usual run. A few of the better ones are: Tops in SF; Science Fiction Quarterly and Fantastic.

Two good S-F books: "Robots Have No Tails" by Lewis Padgett and "Player Piano" by Kurt Vonnegut. Both humorous line.

The officers of IFSB are planning on issuing a 12-page booklet sometime next year with a complete record on all saucer reports that they now have collected. This booklet will not be a regular issue of "Space Review", but a separate issue and will sell for 50c to everyone. Our President, Mr. Bender, will write the foreword with comments throughout by officials of IFSB. The booklet will be entitled: IFSB REPORTS ON THE SAUCERS. If interested, write!

We would like members and officers to send in snapshots of themselves so that when the time comes for us to print pictures in Space Review, we will have the photos available.

MENTION "SPACE REVIEW" when writing to any of above mentioned publications.

This page will be eliminated in future issues, and will be replaced by articles on saucers".

EDITORIAL

In 1492 Columbus discovered a new world after traveling thousands of miles across the great expanse of unknown waters called the Atlantic Ocean. It was a great adventure, yet one that was laughed at, ridiculed, and even spoke of as a "folly".

Here was a small group of men searching for what lay beyond the known, endeavoring to unfold the mysteries of lands that were not supposed to exist. All they had were three small ships laden with provisions that they estimated would last the journey.

The seas were infested with monsters, so the skeptics said, and the world was flat with a dropping off place. Columbus proved these fallacies to be wront, when he landed in the West Indies.

The years directly ahead of us will see another great adventure such as this. A small group of men will assemble in a certain designated place, climb into their ship, a ship vastly different than that of Columbus's time. This ship will be a rocket shop, and its occupants will shoot off into the vast sea of space to find new worlds, new peoples, and new frontiers.

They will be laughed at, they will be ridiculed, and the whole thing will be called the greatest "folly" on earth, but will it be such? Time has proven that impossibilities become realities. The automobile, the airplane, radio, telephone, telegraph, television, and the smashing of the atom are definite proof. All is possible to one who believes,—and I am a sound believer!

FROM THE ASSOCIATE EDITOR'S DESK

The mysteries of space have long fascinated most people on earth. One need not be an astronomer to gaze in awe at that which unfolds before the eyes as we gaze skyward any clear night.

The vastness of space is difficult to explain, even for astronomers. When distances are spoken of it is simpler for learned men to use the term "light years" than miles. The number of celestial bodies suspended in space like our own earth are unknown. The guesses are from millions on up. But they remain just that—guesses.

We who make our home on a mere cinder of matter in the eyes of space, cannot be naive enough to think that intelligent life exists only here. Those who believe that there is a purpose for everything which happens, should agree that these millions of bodies in space must serve more of a purpose than just twinkling brightly on a clear night.

Published quarterly by Albert K. Bender, Editor; Max Krengel, Associate Editor; Printed by Reliable Press, Bridgeport, Conn. Subscription Price: four issues, to members, $1.00; to non members, $1.40 per year. Individual copies $.35. Exclusive publication of the IFSB. P.O Box 241, Bridgeport 2, Conn., U.S.A. Send all news and articles to this address.

SUTTON, WEST VIRGINIA MONSTER MAY BE "COLLIER'S" ROCKET!

Rev. S. L. Daw, Washington, D.C., Representative, IFSB

I have personally photographed flying saucers six times and personally photographed the place where one landed in Charleston, West Virginia. I also talked to two eye-witnesses. I saw and talked to a police officer who was burned by one in Wheeling, West Virginia. My own cousin was the doctor who treated him.

I attempted to photograph one going over Melessa Pass, 3000 feet up in the Blue Ridge mountains, as I was at a height of 2500 feet at Wahala Glen just directly opposite from Melessa Pass. The picture was not too good due to the mist from the mountains.

The object that landed at Charleston, West Virginia was described as a large metal ball, throwing off a white light and after landing, two small men in red emerged from a trap in the top and climbed up a tree to look around. Seeing people watching them, they got back in and took off. We can prove what this was: In the attempt to shoot rockets to the moon, there is a device with the motors on the wings and the body of the device is a jet propelled apparatus which throws off a large metal shaped disc which throws off a red color from the center which when reflected could easily be taken for some sort of a small person. This was described in Collier's magazine of October 11, 1952.

According to the Washington Daily News, the monster seen at Sutton, West Virginia could be the rocket described in Collier magazine. The picture on the cover of the magazine shows a sphere-headed, wide-bottomed, tank-bellied rocket craft spewing out burning hydrazine and nitric acid as it lands hind-end on the moon. The West Virginia people seem to have seen: "An object estimated at 10 feet tall, four feet wide at the bottom ... the size of a man. Two lights flashed from side to side, the machine made a noise like gas escaping, and a sharp sicken... as about." Sounds somewhat the same.

The United States may be expe... with something that the public is not aware of, and it is doing its best to keep ... The age of rocket ships is just around the corner.

CIVILIAN SAUCER INVESTIGATION OF NEW ZEALAND CONTACTS IFSB

The Civilian Saucer Inv... of New Zealand was set up in New Zealand on October 13, 1952. They plan ... ve or disapprove the existence of saucers. It has no affiliation with the Government ... armed forces, or to any society to which its members may belong. Most of the mem... have been studying flying saucer reports for at least five years. They represent all ... sted parties astronomers, scientists, aviators, and the man in the street. The committee ... sists of M... H. Fulton, a sergeant in the R.N.Z.A.F. attached to engineering, who is ... President CSI of NZ; Mr. R. J. Lavaris, a member of the Territorial Air Force, whi... the secre... of CSI of NZ; Mr. G. H. Gilmore, aviation engineering inspector; D I ... ris, a stu... studying for a science degree; and E. J. Greager, an astronomer and eng...

Aims of the committee are ... orrespon... kindred bodies overseas, and to ultimately find the origin of flying ... s and th... aparison.

Mr H. H. Fulton, and Mr R J La... been made members of the International Council of IFSB. We hope to establish ... clations with this society and get a rep... sentati... New Zealand. CSI sent to I... large map of New Zealand showing all spot... saucers have been sighted wi... ry of each sighting. A complete report on th... ll be made in our next issue. t... CSI of New Zealand the best of luck and hop... ney will be a success.

SAUCERS IN THE NEWS

MAYAGUEZ, PUERTO RICO, Oct. 3, 1952—Strange objects were sighted by two persons in Mayaguez on Oct. 3, they were cruising East and were red in color. It was about 10:30 p.m. when they were sighted.

NORWAY AND SWEDEN, Oct. 13, 1952—During October the Norwegian Government stated that a strange object resembling a saucer landed on Norwegian soil. German experts are claiming that the devices are of Russian origin, and the description given by Norway fits the description given by German experts. Stockholm, Sweden, has also been sighting strange objects.

MELBOURNE, AUSTRALIA, Sept. 13, 1952—A young woman sighted a noiseless green ball flying too fast to be a plane or a meteor. She said it smelled like a rotten egg.

STUTTGART, GERMANY, Nov. 1, 1952 —At the recent meeting of the third International Astronautical Congress in Germany where 200 scientists from 12 countries gathered they stated that saucers are not from Mars or any other planet. They said they are merely optical and [illegible].

NEW YORK—A terrific blast took place over a small area of [illegible] N.Y., which broke windows, cracked walks and caused a general panic. There were no planes around or scheduled at that time, Oct. 1952.

INTERNATIONAL AIRPORT, NEW YORK, Oct. 16 1952—A blue flame flashed over International Airport at 7:33 p.m. It was a ball-like object. Hayden Planetarium stated it may have been the [illegible] of a meteor.

YORK, ENGLAND, Sept. 20, 1952—During exercise "Mainbrace" RAF pilots sighted a white object at 10,000 feet. The object was silver in color and circular. It maintained a slow forward speed before beginning to descend, swinging like a pendulum. It followed the aircraft, revolved on its own axis at times, and then took [illegible].

WASHINGTON, D.C., Oct. 16, 1952—The Navy announced that it launched rockets from giant balloons, high above the North Geomagnetic Pole, and sent them to altitudes of about 40 miles. The balloons were as tall as a 10-story building.

PARIS, FRANCE, Oct. 7, 1952 — A flying saucer was sighted over Southern France by two Air France pilots.

WESTERN KOREA FRONT, Oct. 29, 1952 —U.S. troops saw a half-dozen mysterious spark-throwing "cartwheels" over the western front of Korea. They were as the eye sees, 18 inches in diameter, moving in a 15-foot circle.

GAILLAC, SOUTH OF FRANCE, Oct. 29, 1952 —For the second time in two weeks, 20 townspeople of Gaillac saw a series of white circular objects, slightly swollen at the center, spinning across the sky. They were flying in formation of two and were grouped around something that looked like a giant flying cigar. As the objects passed overhead they let fall a sort of string of bright white threads, which settled gently on trees and telephone lines. When the people tried to pick them up, they melted like ice. A police officer who picked up some of the thread said: "It looked like glass wool and it melted away almost as soon as it was touched."

OLORON, FRANCE, Oct. 17, 1952—About a dozen people, including a schoolmaster, saw flying saucers surrounding a long cigar like object flying through a clear sky at about 6,000 feet.

NEW ZEALAND— The clippings and stories from New Zealand are swamping our office and are so numerous that we must devote a whole page to them in our April issue.

For more detailed information on any of the above, please write to IFSB.

Please date your clippings that you send to us, and note the source.

Space Review

Copyright 1953 by ALBERT K. BENDER

VOL. II, No. 1   January, 195_   Bridgeport, Conn., U.S.A.

IFSB OF BRITAIN ORGANIZES

*Capt. E. L. Plunkett Appointed
British Representative.*

The IFSB has finally been organized in Great Britain with retired Capt. E. L. Plunkett, of the 8th Army as British Representative. Mr. Plunkett resides at 71 Chedworth Rd., Horfield, Bristol 7, England. Denis, son of Mr. Plunkett, is the assistant representative, but is now serving his country in the Royal Air Force.

Rep. Plunkett has shown great interest and foresight in forming the IFSB in the British Isles. Numerous articles have appeared in leading newspapers through his efforts. He is planning on using local halls and auditoriums to give lectures and show pictures with the aid of an epidiascope. He also plans to give talks at the local ______ th___ty which is a semiwar veterans type ______ty.

Many people in the British Isles contacted Mr. Plunkett showing great interest in _______ of these people are very learned individuals such as officers in the Armed ____ members of the British Inter-Planetary Society, Aero-Dynamists, newspaper reporters, and flying saucer enthusiasts.

At present Mr. Plunkett is holding weekly meetings at his home, where they discuss IFSB and flying saucers in general. ___ further information about our British representative see page twelve of this see page twelve of this

LUIS LUHRING NAMED
PUERTO RICAN REPRESENTATIVE

Mr. Luis Luhring of Punta Santiago, Puerto Rico, has accepted the position of Representative for the island of Puerto Rico. He will handle all IFSB business in that place. Write to Box 23, Punta Santiago, Puerto Rico. Mr. Luhring is a very capable man and will aid the IFSB greatly

FRANKLIN, INDIANA JOINS EN MASSE

*Business Men and Public Officials Join
IFSB To Form Own City Group.*

The City of Franklin, Indiana, has gone out fully for the IFSB and is now the only city in the world that has the most members in our organization. Through the great efforts and work of Mr. Louis Frahm, business man; Mr. Jack W. Moore, policeman; Mr. Robert Wolf, civilian defense director, and Mr. Dick Campbell, IFSB Representative for Indiana, this great accomplishment was made possible. At this publication, Franklin can claim 20 members with ten from nearly towns, giving a total of 30. Since all this interest has been aroused Mr. Frahm plans to form a city group with their own chairman, secretary and treasurer. Among the members you will find policemen, librarians, mechanics, commercial pilots, business men, bus drivers, ______, etc. The group plans to purchase ______ one of suitable power. In addition ______ they plan to rig up a 3¼ x ¼ G_____ ______ with an optical type view finder ______ door handle on each side ______ ______ng. This is the equipment they plan to start with. Later, if finances permit, they may build a portable radar set.

Franklin and ____ and nearby towns, have been ______ in having had at least four sightings this past summer. Two were witnessed by Mr. Frahm and Mr. Moore. Reports of these sightings are reviewed in this issue of Space Review.

OUR PRESIDENT HEARS FROM
PROF. EINSTEIN

Mr. Al K. Bender, President of IFSB, received a letter from Professor Einstein with this message: "Having no experience and only superficial knowledge in the field ______ I regret not to be able to comply with your requests." Mr. Bender wanted his opinion on the flying saucers. This was ___ Professor ___ reply.

62-83894-336

The International Flying Saucer Bureau

"All is possible to one who believes"

ALBERT K. BENDER
President and Editor

MAX KRENGEL
Vice-Pres. and Treas.

ALAN C. RIEVMAN
Secretary

FRED J. BENDER
Historian

★

INTERNATIONAL
COUNCIL

ROBERT N. WEBSTER
Editor "Fate" Magazine

WILSON "BOB" TUCKER
*Author — Editor of
Science Newslette*

ELLIOTT ROCKMORE
*Editor - Publisher
"Saucer Review"*

GEORGE D. FAWCETT
*Lecturer - Sauceriana
Collection*

STANLEY E. CROW
*Editor Science and
Culture Magazine*

FRANKLIN M. DIETZ
*Editor and Publisher
"Science - Fantasy and
Science Fiction"*

★

BRITISH REPRESENTATIVE

. L. PLUNKETT
Retired Capt. 8th Army

INTERNATIONAL
HEADQUARTERS

P. O. BOX 241

BRIDGEPORT 2, CONN.

U. S. A.

★

Great Britain Branch
71 Chedworth Road
Horfield,
Bristol 7, England

October 26, 1952

Mr.   H. Frahm.
    . . . . t,
Franklin, Indiana

Dear Mr. Frahm:

Once again I am happy to write to you about
and your fine work in helping our organization
grow larger and stronger.

In your last letter you asked what course of action
our club should take in connection with IFSB. I
would suggest the following:

(1.) Appoint a local Chairman of the IFSB in
      Franklin, Indiana. Also appoint a local
      treasurer and secretary.

   . Hold your meetings at least twice a month,
      where you can discuss saucer happenings and
      club activities. Use a local hall, or better
      yet, have the meetings at each others homes.

      If and when you form your own city group, a
      certain portion of the club membership fee
      may be retained by you to help your cause.

      Mr. Dick Cameroi . is an International Officer
      of IFSB and should be paid such respect at all
      our gatherings.

(5). We will do any print card printing you desire or
      cards of similar size.

(6). You can print your club activities in "Space
      Review".

(7). Any contributions from your members to help
      . . . .

ALBERT K. BENDER
President and Editor

MAX KRENOEL
Vice-Pres. and Treas.

ALLAN C. RIEVMAN
Secretary

The
International Flying Saucer Bureau

"All is possible to one who believes"

P. O. BOX 241
BRIDGEPORT 2, CONN.
U. S. A.

)II(

(8). Report to IFSB all reports and sightings in your area. However, first put the sightings before your group and let them judge whether they are authentic or not.

(9). Keep a record of all club members in your area and their activities as far as IFSB in concerned.

(10). Obtain if possible (merely a suggestion), a tape recorder so that you can send actual voice to IFSB headquarters. In this way, I as President, could send messages for you to play at your local meetings. In the future I may even pay your city a visit and attend one of your meetings.

These are all merely suggestions for you to ponder over if you decide to adopt any of them please consult with Indiana Representative, Mr. Campbell. After you have this, get in touch with me at once.

sincerely hope that these suggestions will help you ng some move as to what your local group will do,

Forever Looking Up,

Albert K. Bender
President

TO: MR. A. H. BELMONT   DATE: December 23, 1952

FROM: V. P. KEAY

SUBJECT: PROPOSED STUDY ON THE
         "FLYING SAUCERS" PHENOMENA;
         INTELLIGENCE ADVISORY COMMITTEE

          Reference is made to my memorandum December 5, 1952. You will
recall that at an Intelligence Advisory Committee (IAC) meeting held
December 4, 1952, Dr. H.M. Chadwell, [   ]
directed the members' attention to some aspects of the "flying saucers"
phenomena. He made reference to a presentation of a theory on "saucers"
which had been made by a German atomic scientist and which fact had
caused [   ] to initiate considerable intelligence effort into
the matter. Chadwell also made reference to a recent "saucers" observation in Africa. He did not furnish details on the African observation.

          The Liaison Agent contacted Messrs. Ralph Clerk, Frank Stone,
and Richard Helms, [   ] for the purpose of obtaining additional
details concerning the "saucers" report which centered in Africa. These
individuals furnished information reflecting that a few weeks ago an
explosion of large proportion was picked up on several seismographs and
it was indicated that the explosion was centered in central Africa.
According to Helms and Clark, reports of unknown reliability were received indicating that the explosiong might have emanated from a flying
saucer. More recent reports received from abroad indicate that the
seismographs had picked up an explosion of a meteor. [   ] has requested its Paris office to obtain all available information from French
intelligence sources.

          The Liaison Agent inquired regarding the "saucers" theory which
reportedly was presented by a German atomic scientist. Clark advised
that the report on the scientist had not been received by [   ]

ACTION:

          This matter will be followed by the Liaison Agent for the pur-
pose of obtaining additional details concerning the "saucers" theory
of the German scientist.

SJP:lw

ALL INFORMATION CONTAINED
HEREIN IS UNCLASSIFIED
DATE 5/11/84 BY SP-1 gphfabm
Comp. # 245,536

62-83494-
NOT RECORDED
146 JAN 6 1953

17

January 27, 1953

326

Mr. Robert D. Wolf
19 North Forsythe Street
Franklin, Indiana

Dear Mr. Wolf:

Your letter dated January 20, 1953, has been received, together with enclosures.

Although I would like to be of service in connection with your request, I would like to point out that the FBI is strictly a fact-finding agency and it is not within the scope of its prescribed authority to make evaluations or draw conclusions as to the character or integrity of any organization or individual. I know you will understand the reason for this rule and will appreciate my inability to be of assistance to you in this regard.

The literature and letter you forwarded are being returned.

Sincerely yours,

John Edgar Hoover
Director

COMM - FBI
JAN 2 8 1953
MAILED 20

Enclosures (2)

cc - Indianapolis, with copy of incoming and copy of letter
     signed by Albert K. Bender.
cc - New Haven, with copy of incoming and copy of letter
     signed by Albert K. Bender.
     ATTENTION SAC's: (see next page)

DIC:dep:hkh

Tolson
add
Nichols
Belmont
Clegg
Glavin
Harbo
Rosen
Tracy
Laughlin
Mohr

18

ATTENTION SAC's: *Correspondent also enclosed a copy of the January 19, 1953 issue of "Space Review", the publication of The International Flying Saucer Bureau, indicating the address as Post Office Box 241, Bridgeport, Connecticut. This small periodical contains news of various I.F.S.B. groups throughout the United States and England and news items relating to flying saucers.*

No references can be located in Bufiles on the I.F.S.B.; "Space Review" or Albert K. Bender.

326

RECORDED-84

Date: February 11, 1953

To: Director of Special Investigations
The Inspector General
Department of the Air Force
The Pentagon
Washington 25, D. C.

From: John Edgar Hoover, Director
Federal Bureau of Investigation

Subject: FLYING DISCS
MISCELLANEOUS – INFORMATION CONCERNING

There are attached for your information in the captioned matter a Photostat of a letter dated January 20, 1953, received by this Bureau from Mr. Robert D. Wolf, 19 North Forsythe Street, Franklin, Indiana, with the enclosures referred to therein, and a copy of this Bureau's reply to Mr. Wolf.

No investigation is being conducted by this Bureau in this matter.

Attachment

EHM:eme

COMM – FBI
FEB 11 1953
MAILED 30

FEB 19 1953

C. H. MARCK JR

Mr. Tolson
Mr. Belmont
Mr. Mohr
Mr. Nease
Mr. Parsons
Mr. Rosen
Mr. Tamm
Mr. Trotter
Mr. W.C. Sullivan
Tele. Room
Mr. Holloman
Miss Gandy

7854 North Loma Land Drive
Scottsdale, Arizona
December 7, 1958

FEDERAL BUREAU OF INVESTIGATION
Washington, D. C.

Dear Sir:

I am extremely interested in the "Bender Affair," and I will
be most grateful if you could help clear up the mystery in this
affair. The reason I am writing you is because I have learned
recently that a researcher of the flying saucer mystery said the
FBI is involved in this affair.

A civilian investigating agency was formed in Bridgeport,
Conn., in 1952, to look into the flying saucer mystery by
Albert K. Bender. He called the organization The International
Flying Saucer Bureau. And, during his study of the saucer mystery
Bender ran across something important. This information was
evidently the solution to the mystery for in 1953 Bender stated
bluntly, "I know what the saucers are." Then, "three men in black
suits" silenced him. Even today Bender will not discuss the matter
of his "hush-up" with anyone. However, I have learned that the
secret of the saucers lies the "dreadful underground menace" that
is threatening the world. And, I am also extremely interested in
this "menace."

I have some very important information concerning this
"dreadful underground menace" that I would like to discuss with
Bender very much. For the story concerning this "menace" is
certainly a "hellish Horror" one, which reveals a fantastic
situation, so fantastic, that it would be hardly conceivable by
the public. Yes indeed, I would appreciate it very much if you
could help me get in touch with Bender.

I have also been getting information regarding "certain"
ship tragedies that have occurred on the high seas for a very
long time, and "certain" aircraft accidents and disappearances.
For these tragedies reveal evidence that gives proof that such
a "menace" really "exists."

I certainly will be looking forward in hearing from you.

Sincerely yours

C. H. Marck Jr.

C. H. Marck, Jr.

REC- 37   62 - 23994

DEC 17 1958

1 - Belmont
1 - Donahoe
1 - Wacks

SAC, Phoenix   December 16, 1958

Director, FBI

REC- 37 62 - 83874   398

ALBERT K. BENDER
MISCELLANEOUS - INFORMATION CONCERNING
(Nationalities Intelligence)

    Enclosed is a copy of a letter received from
C. M. Marck, Jr., 7004 North Loma Land Drive, Scottsdale,
Arizona.

    Bufiles contain no information pertaining to the
"Bender Affair" nor to the "hush-up" of Bender as alleged
in paragraph two of the enclosed letter. The only identifiable data in Bureau files on Bender is a letter he wrote
on 10/26/52 on the letterhead of the International Flying
Saucer Bureau to a Mr. L. H. Frahm, Franklin, Indiana, in
which he suggested how Frahm could organize a chapter of
the Saucer Bureau in Franklin. Also in Bufiles is a copy
of the January, 1953, magazine "Space Review" which apparently
was put out by the Saucer Bureau. This magazine contains
numerous articles and squibs concerning the sighting of
flying saucers throughout the world. It does not appear to
have any security significance.

    Unless information in your files would indicate
an interview with Marck is undesirable, immediately contact
him and orally acknowledge the receipt of his letter by the
Bureau. At the same time thoroughly interview Marck and
obtain all data in his possession concerning the "hush-up"
of Bender as well as what part the FBI was alleged to have
played in the "Bender Affair." In the event it is apparent
that the Bureau was not so involved, so advise Marck. Submit
results of this interview to reach the Bureau no later than
12/23/58. It is permissible to advise Marck that the Bureau
is not cognizant of Bender's whereabouts and has no record
of involvement in the "Bender Affair."

Enclosure

NOTE: See cover memo Donahoe to Belmont, same caption,
dated December 12, 1958, JFW:jas.

Tolson _______
Boardman _______
Belmont _______
Mohr _______
Nease _______
Parsons _______
Rosen _______
Tamm _______
Trotter _______
Clayton _______
Tele. Room _______
Holloman _______
Gandy _______

JFW:jas
(6)

JAN 2 1959

MAIL ROOM

DEC 16 1958

STANDARD FORM NO. 64

Office Memorandum • UNITED STATES GOVERNMENT

TO : MR. A. H. BELMONT

FROM : MR. S. B. DONAHOE

SUBJECT: ALBERT K. BENDER
MISCELLANEOUS - INFORMATION CONCERNING
(Nationalities Intelligence)

DATE: December 12, 1958

1 - Belmont
1 - Donahoe
1 - Wacks

Tolson _______
Boardman _____
Belmont _______
Mohr _________
Nease ________
Parsons ______
Rosen ________
Tamm ________
Trotter _______
Clayton ______
Tele. Room ___
Holloman _____
Gandy ________

By letter 12/7/58 Mr. C. H. Marck, Jr., inquired whether we could furnish him any information concerning the "Bender Affair" and advised he was asking the Bureau since he had recently learned that the FBI is involved in this affair. Marck explained that Bender formed the International Flying Saucer Bureau in Bridgeport, Connecticut, in 1952 to look into the flying saucers mystery. In 1953 Bender allegedly stated that he knew what the saucers are. Then according to Marck "three men in black suits" silenced Bender to the extent that even today Bender will not discuss the matter of his "hush-up" with anyone. Marck pointed out he has learned that "the secret of the saucers lies the 'dreadful underground menace' that is threatening the world" and that he has important information concerning this menace. Marck also requested our help in getting in touch with Bender.

Bufiles contain no information on Marck. The only identifiable data in our files on Bender is a letter he wrote on 10/26/52 on the letterhead of the International Flying Saucer Bureau to a Mr. L. H. Frahm, Franklin, Indiana, in which he suggested how Frahm could organize a chapter of the Saucer Bureau in Franklin. Also in Bufiles is a copy of the January, 1953, magazine "Space Review" which apparently was put out by the Saucer Bureau. This magazine contains numerous articles and squibs concerning the sighting of flying saucers throughout the world. It does not appear to have any security significance.

RECOMMENDATION:

There is a possibility that Marck may be suffering from delusions; however, in view of the fact that he stated the FBI is involved in a matter of which we are not cognizant as well as the implications in his description of the "hush-up" of Bender, it is recommended he be interviewed and all information in his possession concerning this incident be obtained so that we can decide whether the facts warrant investigation. At the same time his letter will be orally acknowledged.

A letter to Phoenix is enclosed. REC-37 62-83894-398

Enclosure
JFW:jas
(4)

DEC 17 1958

STANDARD FORM NO. 64

Office Memorandum · UNITED STATES GOVERNMENT

TO : DIRECTOR, FBI   DATE: 12/19/58

FROM : SAC, PHOENIX (62-667)

SUBJECT: ALBERT K. BENDER
MISCELLANEOUS - INFORMATION CONCERNING
(Nationalities Intelligence)

Re Bureau letter 12/16/58.

On 12/19/58, CLAUDE HAROLD MARCK, JR., 7834 No. Loma
Land Drive, Scottsdale, Arizona, stated to SAs GEORGE
HOLLINGSWORTH and WILLIAM M. DREW that he had a hobby
of gathering information concerning flying saucers and
also gathering information concerning mysteries of the
sea. He stated that any literature written he obtains
in order to pursue this hobby. He referred agents to
books written by Major DONALD E. KEYHOE entitled
"Flying Saucers from Outer Space" and a book entitled
"Flying Saucers Conspiracy." Both of these books were
published by Henry Holt Company, 383 Madison, New York, 17,
New York. Major KEYHOE is a retired Major of the U. S.
Marine Corps.

Concerning the "Bender Affair", he referred agents to
the book entitled "They Knew Too Much About Flying
Saucers", written by GRAY BARKER and published by
University Books Publisher, April, 1956, third
printing June, 1956. According to MARCK, GRAY BARKER
resides at Clarksberg, West Virginia, P. O. Box 2228
and is a person with whom MARCK corresponds concerning
flying saucers as BARKER is alleged to have a civilian
investigative agency handling investigations
concerning flying saucers.

MARCK related that he has corresponded with various
harbor masters and the U. S. Navy relative to the
"dreadful underground menace which relates to the
disappearance of crew and passengers of various ships
found floundering in the open seas out of control."
He stated that BARKER has also shown interest in this
subject matter, however, was unable to furnish any
further amplifying details. The "Bender Affair" is
related in the book published by BARKER.

(2) - Bureau (AM)
1 - Phoenix
WMD/mdc
(3)

COPIES DESTROYED
NOV 19 1964

Agents observed at the time they contacted the residence of MARCK, while he was absent therefrom, that his sister, SHIRLEY E. MARCK, carried on exclusive conversation concerning her brother relating that he had been taken out of high school while living in Denver, Colorado, and had been in the service until several months ago. She stated that her brother never had an opportunity since then to complete his schooling and that as of the present time, he was 33 years of age. This information was reiterated several times by her while waiting the arrival of her brother who was with his parents on a local shopping tour. After conversation with MARCK, it was apparent to agents that he is obsessed with gathering information concerning flying saucers and mysteries of the sea. He was admonished severely by his mother for having written to the Bureau without her knowledge.

Inquiry was made as to the length of time MARCK spent in the U. S. Army and he was unable to furnish the duration of his enlistment and date of discharge nor furnish his serial number. MARCK made available his discharge paper reflecting that he was inducted in 1943 and discharged in 1946 as Private First Class, Army Serial No. 37-703-300. His discharge papers showed that he attended East High School for a period of two years and that he was born 1/21/25.

After conversation with MARCK, it was apparent that the only reason he wrote to the Bureau was in an effort to locate the present whereabouts of ALBERT K. BENDER and he and his family were informed that this Bureau was unable to institute an investigation to ascertain the whereabouts of BENDER.

From the admonishment given him by his mother for writing letters to such agencies as the FBI, it would appear that CLAUDE HAROLD MARCK is a "chronic", living in a dream world of flying saucers and stories of the sea. He was informed that the agents' contact was an acknowledgment of the Bureau's receipt of his letter.

Nofurther investigation is being made in this matter.

SAC, Phoenix (62-667)   December 30, 1958

Director, FBI

ALBERT K. BENDER
MISCELLANEOUS - INFORMATION CONCERNING
(Nationalities Intelligence)

Flying Discs

     Reurlet 12/19/58. In paragraph two thereof
reference is made to a book written by Gray Barker and
published by University Books Publisher entitled "They
Knew Too Much About Flying Saucers." Reference books
at the Seat of Government fail to reflect the location
of this publisher and since the Bureau is desirous of
obtaining a copy of this book, it is requested that you
recontact Claude Marck, Jr., to obtain the correct
address of the publisher. In the event Marck volunteers
to make a copy of this book available, it is permissible
for you to accept same and furnish it to the Bureau.

                                      62-83899- 460

              EX-12   REC-32
                                   23 DEC 31 1958

JFW:jac
(4)

          NOTE: By letter 12/7/58 Marck inquired whether we
could furnish him any data concerning the "Bender Affair."
He explained that Bender formed the International Flying
Saucer Bureau in Connecticut in 1952 to look into the flying
saucer mystery. In 1953 Bender allegedly stated he knew what
the saucers are; then, according to Marck, "Three men in black
suits" silenced Bender to the extent that even today Bender
will not discuss the matter of his "hush-up" with anyone. Marck
explained that he recently learned that the FBI is involved in
the "Bender Affair." On 12/19/58 Marck was interviewed to
obtain all information in his possession concerning the "hush-up"
of Bender as well as what part the FBI was alleged to have
played in the "Bender Affair." Concerning the "Bender Affair"
he referred the interviewing Agents to the book set out above. In
addition to information regarding this incident it is possible
this book may contain other data of interest. Accordingly, not
only to resolve this matter but also to ascertain whether any
allegations of interest to the Bureau are contained in the book,
we should if possible obtain a copy. Upon receipt, it will be
reviewed with the Bureau's interest in mind.

1 - J. F. Wacks

SAC, Chicago   January 22, 1959

Director, FBI (62-83894)-401

ALBERT K. BENDER
MISCELLANEOUS - INFORMATION CONCERNING
(Nationalities Intelligence)

The Bureau desires to obtain a copy of the book written by Gray Barker entitled "They Knew Too Much About Flying Saucers." Reportedly, this book was published by University Books, Inc., 806 Dempster Street, Evanston, Illinois. Contact this publishing house and if possible, obtain a copy of this book.

<u>NOTE:</u>

By letter 12/7/58 Claude Marck, Jr., Phoenix, Arizona, wrote the Bureau inquiring about the "Bender Affair." He explained that Bender formed the International Flying Saucer Bureau in Connecticut in 1952 to look into the flying saucer mystery. In 1953 Bender stated he knew what the saucers are; then, according to Marck, "3 men in black suits" silenced Bender to the extent that even today Bender will not discuss the matter of his "hush-up" with anyone. Marck was interviewed 12/19/58 and with respect to the "Bender Affair" he referred the interviewing Agents to the book set out above. In addition to information regarding this incident it is possible this book may contain other data of interest. Accordingly, Phoenix was instructed to reinterview Marck to obtain a copy of the book and/or the true name of the publisher which Marck had stated was "University Books Publisher," with no address indicated. In Phoenix letter 1/5/59 it is pointed out that Marck has moved to Denver, exact address not available but that University Books, Inc., is located at the above address.

JFW:jac
(4)

MAILED 27
JAN 22 1959
COMM-FBI

MAIL ROOM ☐   TELETYPE UNIT ☐

Office Memorandum • UNITED STATES GOVERNMENT

TO : DIRECTOR, FBI   DATE: 1/5/59

FROM : SAC, PHOENIX (62-667)

SUBJECT: ALBERT K. BENDER
MISCELLANEOUS - INFORMATION CONCERNING
(Nationalities Intelligence)

Re Bulet to Phoenix dated 12/30/58.

CLAUDE MARCK, Jr. and his family have moved to Denver, Colorado and their exact address is not available.

It was determined through the Phoenix Public Library that University Books, Inc., is located at 806 Dempster Street, Evanston, Illinois.

2 - Bureau
1 - Phoenix

WMD/hpw
(3)

REC-68

EX-128